SUPER
SANDCASTLE
State Stories

Rocky's Outdoor
Adventure

~ A Story About Colorado ~

Written by Colleen Dolphin
Illustrated by Bob Doucet

Consulting Editor, Diane Craig, M.A./Reading Specialist

A Division of ABDO
ABDO
Publishing Company

Published by ABDO Publishing Company, a division of ABDO, P.O.
Box 398166, Minneapolis, Minnesota 55439. Copyright © 2011 by
Abdo Consulting Group, Inc. International copyrights reserved in
all countries. No part of this book may be reproduced in any form
without written permission from the publisher. Super SandCastle™
is a trademark and logo of ABDO Publishing Company.

Printed in the United States of America, North Mankato, Minnesota
112010
012011

 PRINTED ON RECYCLED PAPER

Editor: Liz Salzmann
Content Developer: Nancy Tuminelly
Cover and Interior Design: Anders Hanson, Mighty Media
Production: Colleen Dolphin, Oona Gaarder-Juntti, Mighty Media
Photo Credits: David Amirault, Scott Brim, Captain ZipLine Tours,
Wayne Davis, Footwarrior, Michael Greiner, Chris Lott, iStockphoto/
David Parsons, David Merten, Colorado State Parks, Museum of
Western Colorado, One Mile Up, Quarter-dollar coin image from the
United States Mint, Shutterstock, William Van

Library of Congress Cataloging-in-Publication Data

Dolphin, Colleen, 1979-
  Rocky's outdoor adventure : a story about Colorado / Colleen
Dolphin ; illustrated by Bob Doucet.
     p. cm. -- (Fact & fable: state stories)
  ISBN 978-1-61714-684-8
  1. Colorado--Juvenile literature. I. Doucet, Bob, ill. II. Title.
  F776.3.D65 2011
  978.8--dc22

                      2010022166

TABLE OF CONTENTS

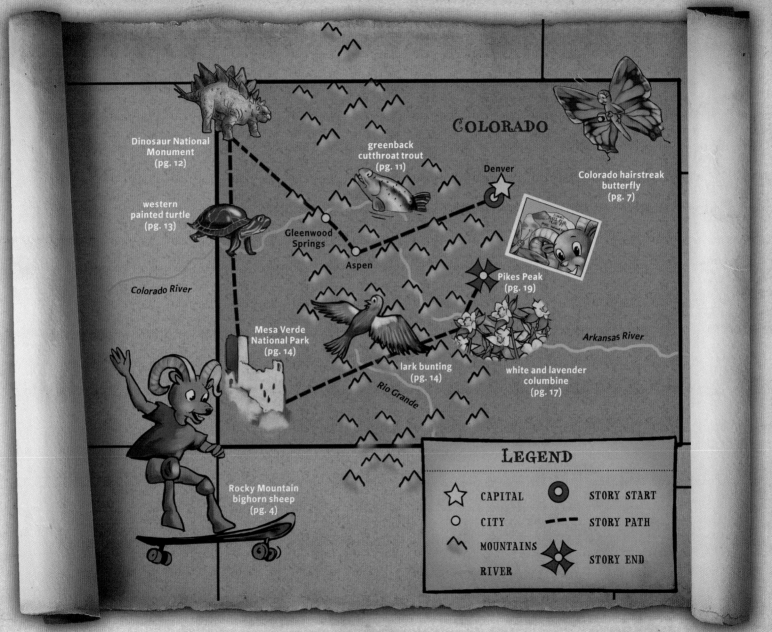

COLORADO

Dinosaur National Monument (pg. 12)

greenback cutthroat trout (pg. 11)

Denver

Colorado hairstreak butterfly (pg. 7)

western painted turtle (pg. 13)

Gleenwood Springs

Aspen

Colorado River

Pikes Peak (pg. 19)

Mesa Verde National Park (pg. 14)

lark bunting (pg. 14)

Arkansas River

white and lavender columbine (pg. 17)

Rio Grande

Rocky Mountain bighorn sheep (pg. 4)

LEGEND

☆ CAPITAL   ◎ STORY START

○ CITY   - - - STORY PATH

⋀ MOUNTAINS   ✧ STORY END

RIVER

Rocky Mountain Bighorn Sheep

Bighorn sheep have huge horns. A **male's** horns can weigh up to 30 pounds (14 kg)! **Females** have horns too. But they are much smaller. Bighorn sheep live in herds and are very good climbers.

Rocky's Outdoor Adventure

I t was a cool and sunny spring day in Denver. Rocky, a bighorn sheep, is hanging out with his friend Sonia at the Denver Skate Park. Rocky loves sports and being outdoors.

Rocky is working on a new trick when Sonia runs over to him waving a piece of paper.

"Check out this flyer," says Sonia. "There's an Ultimate Sports Challenge going on all over Colorado. It starts tomorrow!"

"Challenge Yourself at the Ultimate Sports Challenge!" Rocky reads out loud. "Hike, bike, **raft**, ski, and rock climb throughout Colorado."

"Oh, I'm totally doing this!" Rocky exclaims.

"It sounds like an great time," says Sonia "But are you sure you can do it?"

"Of course I can!" says Rocky. "You'll see!" He runs home to pack and get ready.

Denver

Denver is the capital of Colorado. It's nicknamed the "Mile-High City." That's because its official **elevation** is exactly 1 mile (2 km) above sea level! Denver was founded in 1858 during the Pikes Peak Gold Rush.

Red Rocks Amphitheater

Red Rocks Amphitheater is in Red Rocks Park. Many outdoor **concerts** are held there. Huge rocks surround the stage. More than 9,000 people can sit around and between the rocks!

The next morning Rocky biked to the Red Rocks Amphitheater. That's where the race will start.

When he arrives there is a huge **celebration** going on. Everyone is waiting for the challenge to begin.

Rocky starts to feel nervous. Then he hears a quiet voice behind him say, "Hello." He turns around and sees a **butterfly**.

"I'm Aponi," she says.

"Hi Aponi, I'm Rocky."

Just then Brianna Bear announces, "It's time to get started! Everyone please take a seat."

Aponi and Rocky sit together. They are given a map and instructions. "I need to have my picture taken at each challenge," says Rocky.

"I can take the pictures for you," says Aponi.

"Totally!" says Rocky "We'll make a great team!"

Colorado Hairstreak Butterfly

The Colorado hairstreak **butterfly** is the state **insect**. Its wings are purple, black, and orange. It finds food in gambel oak trees.

Aspen

Aspen was founded as a silver mining camp. It got its name because of the many aspen trees in the area! Today it is a ski **resort** and **tourist** center. Many famous people have vacation homes in Aspen.

"The first challenge is to go downhill skiing at Snowmass Ski Area," says Rocky. "Let's head for Aspen."

"I'm right behind you!" says Aponi.

Rocky and Aponi arrive in Aspen a few days later.

Rocky picks out some skis. Then he rides to the top of the mountain. Aponi follows with the camera.

"Are you nervous?" asks Aponi.

"A little," says Rocky. "But ready or not, here I go!"

Aponi snaps a picture as Rocky skis down the mountain.

"Wow," thinks Aponi. "That looks like fun!"

Skiing

Skiing is very popular in Colorado. Each year, about 12 million people take winter vacations to Colorado. The state receives more than 300 inches of snow each winter!

Glenwood Springs

The Colorado River and the Roaring Fork River meet in Glenwood Springs. **Rafting**, **kayaking**, and fishing are very popular. About 8,500 people live in Glenwood Springs.

White water rafting in Glenwood Springs is next on the list. Rocky and Aponi eat a big breakfast and go on their way.

"That Denver omelet was the best!" says Aponi. "I'm so full!"

"Me too," says Rocky. "We'll feel better after some exercise. Let's go!"

They find a small rafting company on the Colorado River. "This looks like a good place to go white water rafting," says Rocky.

Denver Omelet

2 eggs

2 tablespoons milk

1 tablespoon butter

½ green pepper, chopped

½ cup shredded cheese

1 slice ham, chopped

½ tomato, sliced

Beat the eggs and milk together in a bowl. Melt the butter in skillet. Pour the egg mixture into skillet. Let it cook for about 2 minutes. Quickly put the remaining ingredients on one half of the egg. Fold the egg over the ingredients. Cook the omelet for about 30 seconds on each side.

"Who's in charge here?" asks Rocky.

"Down here!" they hear a voice say. Aponi and Rocky look over the edge of the dock. There is a trout with a **raft**.

"Are you two ready for an adventure?" asks the fish. "I'm Logan, your guide. Jump aboard!"

Rocky jumps onto the raft. He puts on his safety gear, and off they go.

"This is so exciting!" yells Rocky. Aponi snaps a picture.

Greenback Cutthroat Trout

There are not as many greenback cutthroat trout as there once were. In fact, scientists in the 1930s thought they were **extinct**. But a group of them was discovered in 1957! It is the state fish of Colorado.

11

Dinosaur National Monument

There are hundreds of dinosaur bones at Dinosaur National Monument. Millions of years ago, floods washed the dinosaurs into the area. Today their **fossils** are covered with layers of rock. Some of the rock has been carefully removed. That's so people can see the bones!

Hiking at Dinosaur National Monument is the next challenge.

"This place is great!" says Rocky when they get there. "I can't wait to see some dinosaur fossils. How cool is that?"

"I know!" says Aponi.

Rocky and Aponi walk along the hiking path.

"Look, there's a **fossil**!" says Aponi.

"Wow! I wonder what kind it is," says Rocky.

"It's part of a stegosaurus," replies a turtle sunning itself nearby. "I'm Jacob. I can show you around if you want."

"That would be great!" says Rocky. The three of them hike and **explore** the rest of the day. Aponi takes a lot of pictures.

Western Painted Turtle

The western painted turtle is the Colorado state **reptile**. It lives in ponds, lakes, swamps, and slow rivers. The skin on its head, neck, feet, and tail are striped. The red and yellow stripes look hand painted!

13

Lark Bunting

The lark bunting is the state bird of Colorado. Lark buntings spend a lot of time on the ground. They even build their nests in the grass! They eat **insects** and seeds.

The next day Aponi and Rocky thank Jacob and start their journey to Mesa Verde National Park.

"We need to hike to Cliff Palace," says Aponi looking at the map.

"Did you say Cliff Palace?" asks a lark bunting flying above them. "It's is an ancient Pueblo city. That's where I'm headed. I'm Ava. Follow me!"

When they get there, Rocky says, "I had no idea this was even here. I'm so glad we met you, Ava. Thanks for leading us here."

"You're welcome," says Ava. "Enjoy your time here, and be careful!"

"We will!" reply Aponi and Rocky.

"Smile, Rocky," says Aponi, taking his picture.

Cliff Palace

Cliff dwellings are rooms built into the sides of cliffs. Cliff Palace is the largest cliff dwelling in North America. It has 150 rooms! Ancient Pueblo people built Cliff Palace around the 1300s.

15

Royal Gorge Bridge

The Royal Gorge Bridge is 955 feet (291 m) above the Arkansas River. The bridge is 1,260 feet (384 m) long! It hangs from tall towers. Many people visit the bridge each year.

The next day Rocky and Aponi head to Pikes Peak, the final challenge.

"I think we should stop by the Royal Gorge Bridge on our way," says Rocky. "It has some great views of the Arkansas River."

"We can't miss that!" says Aponi. "Let's go!"

When they arrive Rocky is very excited to walk across the bridge. "It's wonderful!" says Rocky.

"You're brave to be up so high without wings," says Aponi.

"I just think about how cool the view is," says Rocky. "Look at the mountains! I can even see flowers!"

Aponi and Rocky look at the view for a long time. Then Aponi says, "Okay, we'd better get going."

White and Lavender Columbine

The white and lavender columbine is the state flower. It is also called the Rocky Mountain columbine. Many of them grow around the Rocky Mountains. They are 2 to 10 inches (5 to 25 cm) tall.

Colorado Blue Spruce

The Colorado blue spruce is the Colorado state tree. It is 82 to 98 feet (25 to 30 m) tall. It grows well along streams in mountain valleys. It is very common near the Rocky Mountains.

Pretty soon they arrive at Pikes Peak.

"The last challenge is to go rock climbing on Pikes Peak," says Rocky. "My specialty!"

"Let's rest by this spruce tree before you begin," suggests Aponi. "You need to have a lot of **energy** before you start. This is the hardest challenge yet."

After awhile Rocky says, "Okay, I'm ready. Wish me luck."

"Good luck!" replies Aponi.

Rocky starts to climb. It is a hard climb, but he can hear Aponi cheering for him. He can't wait to tell Sonia all about his adventure. And he'll have the pictures to prove he finished.

Finally he reaches the top of the climb.

"You did it!" says Aponi.

Rocky smiles and Aponi takes his picture.

THE END

Pikes Peak

Pikes Peak is in the eastern Rocky Mountains. It towers above the city of Colorado Springs. Pikes Peak is more than 14,000 feet (4,200 m) tall. Mountains that tall are called "fourteeners." There are 54 "fourteeners" in Colorado.

COLORADO AT A GLANCE

Abbreviation: CO

Capital: Denver

Largest city: Denver

Statehood: August 1, 1876 (38th state)

Area: 104,094 square miles (269,602 sq km) (8th-largest state)

Nickname: Centennial State

Motto: Nil sine Numine — Nothing without the Deity

State flower: white and lavender columbine

State tree: Colorado blue spruce

State bird: lark bunting

State reptile: western painted turtle

State Animal: Rocky Mountain bighorn sheep

State song: "Where the Columbines Grow," "Rocky Mountain High"

STATE SEAL

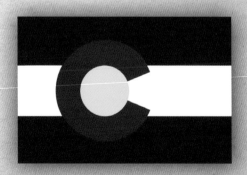

STATE FLAG

STATE QUARTER

The Colorado quarter shows the Rocky Mountains in the background with some evergreen trees surrounding them. The words, "Colorful Colorado" are on a banner at the bottom.

WHAT DO YOU KNOW?

How well do you remember the story? Match the pictures to the
questions below! Then check your answers at the bottom of the page!

a. Red Rocks
Amphitheater

b. Ava the lark
bunting

c. Denver
omelets

d. skiing

e. columbines

f. Pikes Peak

1. Where do Rocky and Aponi meet?

2. What is the first challenge?

3. What do Rocky and Aponi eat for
   breakfast?

4. Who leads Rocky and Aponi to Cliff
   Palace?

5. What do Rocky and Aponi see from the
   Royal Gorge Bridge?

6. What does Rocky climb for the final
   challenge?

What to Do in Colorado

1 BE IN FOUR STATES AT ONCE!
Four Corners Monument, Southwest corner of Colorado

2 VISIT A MUSEUM
Museum of Western Colorado, Grand Junction

3 ENJOY RECREATIONAL ACTIVITIES
Vail Recreation District, Vail

4 LEARN ABOUT LOCOMOTIVES
Colorado Railroad Museum, Golden

5 EXPLORE A CAVE
Cave of the Winds, Manitou Springs

6 RIDE A TRAIN TO A MOUNTAINTOP
Pikes Peak Cog Railway, Colorado Springs

7 EXPERIENCE A ZIP LINE ADVENTURE!
Captain Zip Line Adventure Tours, Salida

8 CATCH A FISH!
Lathrop State Park, Walsenburg

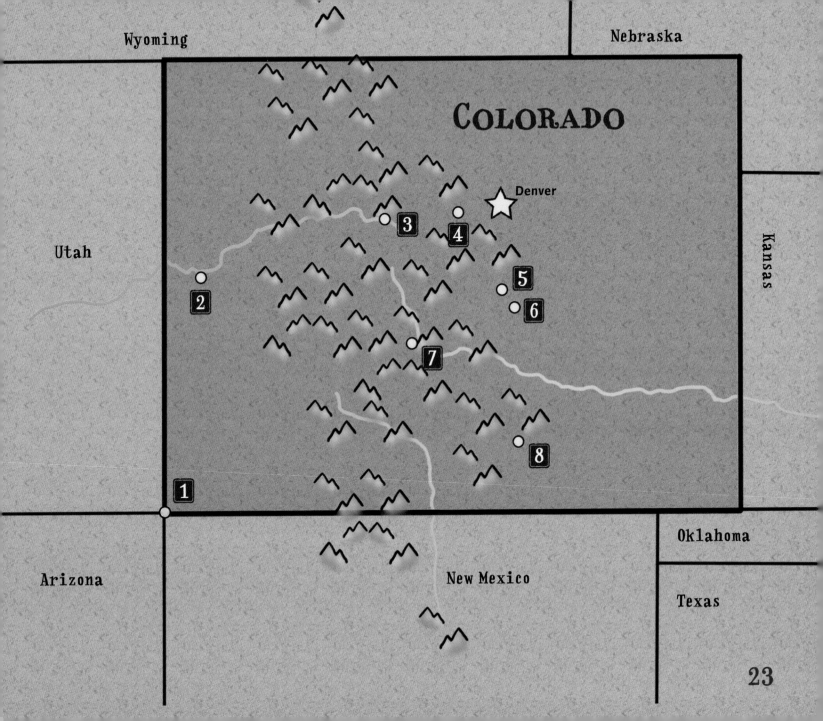

Wyoming

Nebraska

COLORADO

Denver

Utah

Kansas

3

4

2

5

6

7

1

8

Oklahoma

Arizona

New Mexico

Texas

23

GLOSSARY

butterfly – a thin insect with large brightly colored wings.

celebration – a party or festival held to mark a special occasion.

concert – a musical performance or show.

elevation – how high something is.

energy – the ability to move, work, or play hard without getting tired.

explore – to learn about a place by walking all around it.

extinct – no longer existing.

female – being of the sex that can produce eggs or give birth. Mothers are female.

fossil – the remains or imprint of something that lived a long time ago.

insect – a small creature with two or four wings, six legs, and a body with three sections.

kayak – to paddle a kayak, which is a small, narrow boat.

male – being of the sex that can father offspring. Fathers are male.

raft – a flat boat or mat used to float on water. *Rafting* is when you ride a raft down a river.

reptile – a cold-blooded animal, such as a snake, turtle, or alligator, that moves on its belly or on very short legs.

resort – a place where people go on vacation to rest or do fun activities.

tourist – a person who visits a place for fun or to learn something.